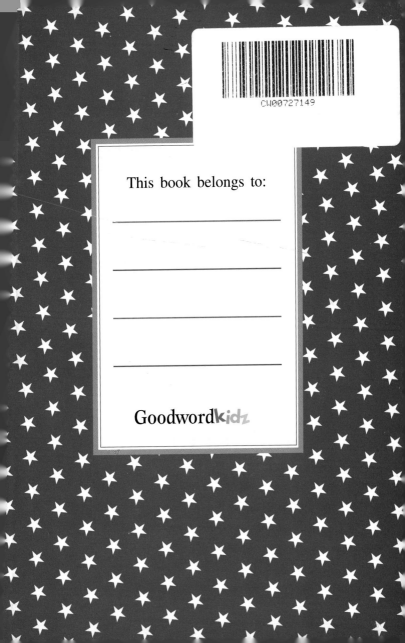

This book belongs to:

_____

_____

_____

_____

Goodword kidz

Goodword Books Pvt. Ltd.
P. B. No. 3244, Nizamuddin West, New Delhi-110 013
E-mail: info@goodwordbooks.com
Illustrated by Achla Anand
First published 2004
Reprinted 2007
Printed in India
© Goodword Books 2007

www.goodwordbooks.com

FAVOURITE TALES FROM THE QURAN

TWO TALES:

Faith in Allah
The Beloved Son

Saniyasnain Khan

Goodword**kidz**
Helping you build a family of faith

Faith in Allah

Long long ago, about 4000 years ago, in the faraway lands of Iraq a child whose name was Ibrahim (Abraham) ﷺ was born in the village of Ur.

He was gracious, kind and pure in faith.
Allah gave him wisdom when he was
still a child. Allah was so pleased with
him that He made him his best friend.

Ibrahim's desire to find the truth grew.
One night, while looking at the sky,
Ibrahim ﷺ saw a particularly bright star.

"This is my Lord," he said. But when it set, he said. "I do not love that which fades."

After seeing the same thing happen with the moon and the sun, Ibrahim ﷺ said: "I will turn my face to Him who has created the heavens and the earth, and live a righteous life..."

12

When Ibrahim ﷺ began his preachings about the creator of the heavens and the earth, the people became very angry, and tried to kill him by burning him alive.

A huge heap of firewood was piled up and set alight. The people shouted: "Death to Ibrahim! Burn him!" As the bright red flames leaped up, Ibrahim عليه السلام felt no fear, as his faith in Allah was very strong and he knew that the people were wrong.

As soon as the fire was at its hottest, they picked up the Prophet Ibrahim ﷺ and threw him into it. But Allah commanded: "O fire, be cool and peaceful for Ibrahim." A miracle took place, and the fire, instead of burning Ibrahim ﷺ, became a cool safe place for him. The people could hardly believe their eyes! They became spechless.

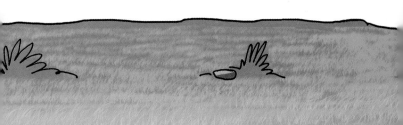

The moral of the story is that faith in Allah is the only thing that can save a believer in this world and the world to come.

The Beloved Son

SURAH AS-SAFFAT 37:102-111

The Prophet Ibrahim (Abraham) عليه السلام lived long long ago—about 4000 years ago. He was good, kind and pure in faith. His family lived in a beautiful valley, now known as Makkah.

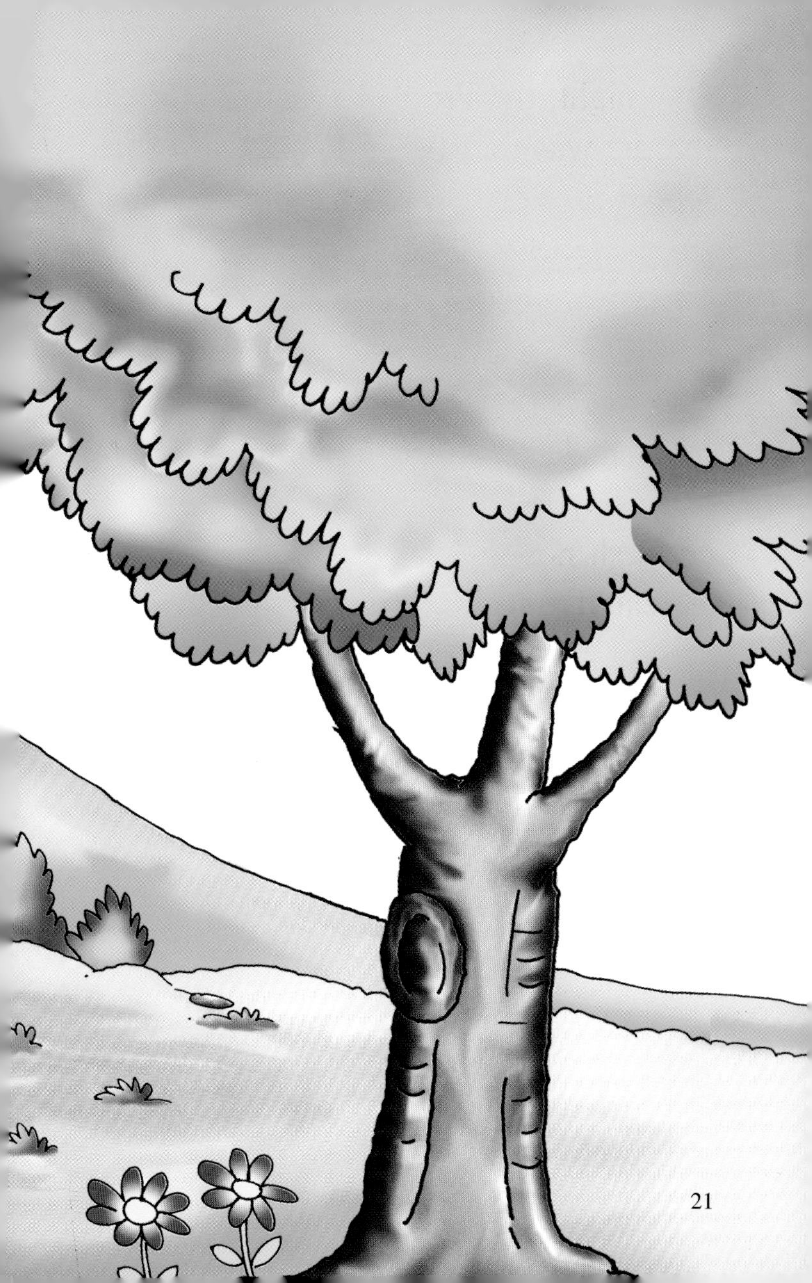

One night, the Prophet Ibrahim ﷺ dreamt that he was sacrificing his beloved son, Ismail ﷺ. This was an order from his Lord. He told Ismail ﷺ that this was an order from his Lord. Ismail ﷺ was a brave boy, and ready to obey. He at once said to his father, "Do as you are commanded, father." Ibrahim ﷺ took his son away to sacrifice him in a valley near Makkah now known as Mina. Satan appeared and tried to stop him.

But the Prophet Ibrahim عليه السلام threw stones at Satan. Little Ismail عليه السلام and his mother did so too.

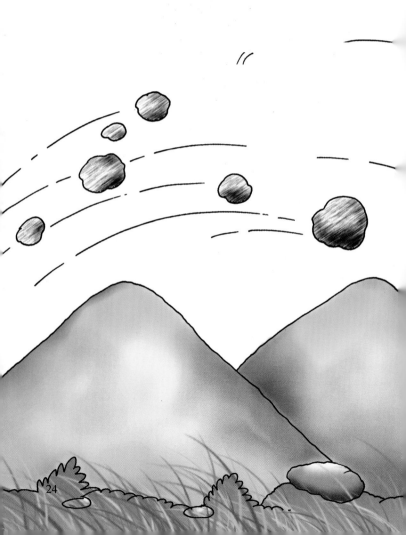

The Prophet Ibrahim ﷺ gently placed his son on the ground and tied a handkerchief around his eyes so that he could not see his beloved son while doing as his Lord said.

25

But as Ibrahim ﷺ picked up his knife, Allah sent the angel Jibril (Gabriel) down with a ram. "Sacrifice this ram—not Ismail," said Jibril.

Allah was so pleased with the Prophet Ibrahim's readiness to sacrifice his beloved son, that He commanded the believers to observe this day as Id al-Adha or the Feast of Sacrifice. Every year Muslims sacrifice an animal to remember the Prophet Ibrahim's trust in Allah.

Believers, too, should be ready to part with their wealth, if that is what Islam needs. The Quran says:

"Truly, my prayers, my sacrifice, my life and my death all belong to Allah, the Lord of the Worlds".

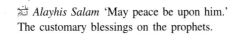 *Alayhis Salam* 'May peace be upon him.'
The customary blessings on the prophets.